United States
Department of
Agriculture

Forest Service

Pacific Northwest
Research Station

General Technical Report
PNW-GTR-839

August 2011

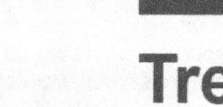

Trends in Global Shipping and the Impact on Alaska's Forest Products

Joseph A. Roos, Allen M. Brackley, and Daisuke Sasatani

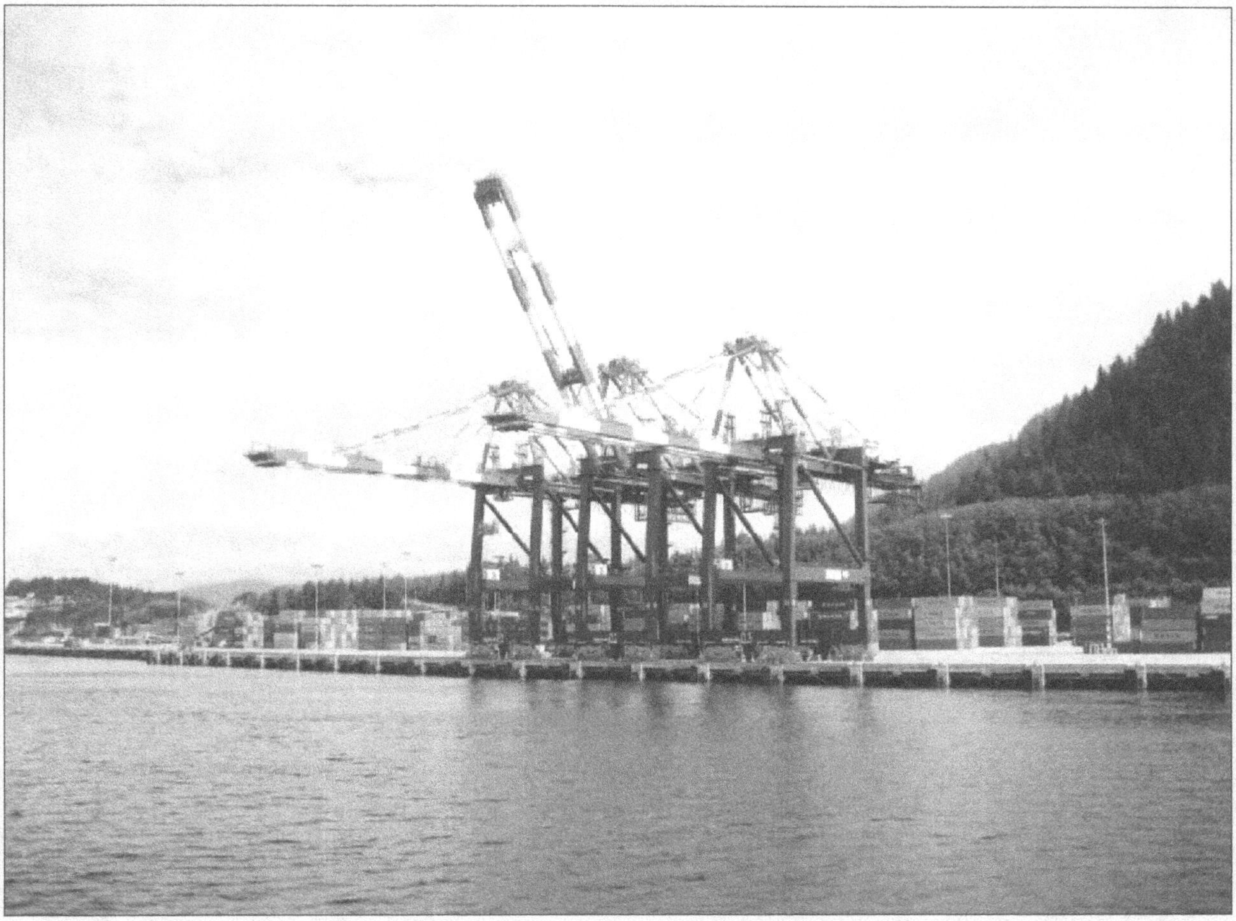

Authors

Joseph A. Roos is a research associate and **Daisuke Sasatani** is a research assistant, University of Washington, Seattle, WA 98105; **Allen M. Brackley** is a research forester, U.S. Department of Agriculture, Forest Service, Pacific Northwest Research Station, Alaska Wood Utilization Research and Development Center, 204 Siginaka Way, Sitka, AK 99835.

Cover: Prince Rupert Container Terminal, British Columbia, Canada. Photo by Allen M. Brackley.

Abstract

Roos, Joseph A.; Brackley, Allen M.; Sasatani, Daisuke. 2011. Trends in global shipping and the impact on Alaska's forest products. Gen. Tech. Rep. PNW-GTR-839. Portland, OR: U.S. Department of Agriculture, Forest Service, Pacific Northwest Research Station. 30 p.

Traditionally, there has been a strong forest products trade between Alaska and Asia. This trade relationship has developed owing to Alaska's proximity to Asia and, in the past, an abundance of high-quality timber. Although forest products markets in North America remain soft, markets in Asia are growing. However, to benefit from Asia's growing forest products market, it is important to understand the concepts of global shipping including containerization, intermodal transport, non vessel operating common carriers, and freight forwarders. One key development that could have a major impact on Alaska's forest products trade is the opening of the Port of Prince Rupert (British Columbia) in 2007. The Port of Prince Rupert ships lumber, logs, and wood pellets to Asia and is much closer to southeast Alaska than are the ports of Seattle and Tacoma. The Prince Rupert port is also 1 day closer to Asia. Despite Prince Rupert's proximity to Alaska, however, there is still no regularly scheduled barge service between the Port of Prince Rupert and southeast Alaska. Potential connections that may develop are examined in this paper. This paper also examines the changing concepts of global shipping and how they affect Alaska's forest products industry.

Keywords: Global shipping, forest products trade, lumber exports, log exports.

Contents

Introduction

Since the closing of the pulp mills in Sitka and Ketchikan, the relatively small sawmills in southeast Alaska have been producing factory and shop lumber and specialty products (Brackley and Haynes 2008) that require a supply of old-growth timber. Dimension lumber is a byproduct of these mills. One of the major issues facing southeast Alaska's sawmills is securing a continuing supply of timber. According to a recent sawmill processing-capacity study, southeast Alaska's forest products industry was estimated to be using approximately 13 percent of mill capacity (Brackley and Crone 2009). This report shows that there is ample processing capacity to increase supply to Asian markets. However, there needs to be a steady timber source to supply southeast Alaska's mills. Demand for Asia's forest products is growing faster than that for North America's, presenting an opportunity to use Alaska's excess mill capacity, if the producers recognize the requirements of the Asian markets.

Alaska has increased its kiln-dried lumber capacity, opening segments of the Asian markets that do not accept green lumber. In 2000, Alaska had an installed kiln capacity of only about 94,000 board feet, limiting its ability to export lumber to Asia and the Lower 48 States. To increase lumber kiln drying capacity, a federal grant program was initiated, and by 2004, Alaska had an estimated 220,000 board feet of kiln drying capacity (Nicholls et al. 2006).

In addition to increasing kiln-dried lumber capacity, Alaska's forest products industry further progressed by establishing three Western Wood Products Association (WWPA) registered grade marks: Alaska Hem, Alaska Yellow Cedar, and Alaska Spruce (WWPA 2005). These registered grade marks were the result of an in-grade testing program conducted by the Ketchikan Wood Technology Center. The results showed that the strength values of these species differ from those of species in the Lower 48 States. Product differentiation is a key principle of marketing; the establishment of these WWPA registered grade marks allows Alaska forest products to be differentiated from lumber in other regions. These registered grade marks along with Alaska's ability to provide Asian markets with kiln-dried lumber has opened opportunities such as supplying the Japanese market with lamstock lumber (Roos et al. 2008a).

Logs from privately owned lands are the major forest product exported from southeast Alaska (Brackley and Haynes 2008). The total volume of specialty products and lumber available for export from the southeast region will always be small in relation to the total volumes traded in the Asian markets. However, the economic value from these exports is vitally important to maintaining the health of small

One of the major issues facing southeast Alaska's sawmills is securing a continuing supply of timber.

1

rural communities of the region. The characteristics of the future wood supply, if any, will be a critical factor in determining the future markets for the small mills of the region.

Current Trade Patterns

International trade is a major component of Alaska's forest products industry. The importance of Asia to Alaska's forest products industry is illustrated by the total value of forest products exported by Alaska. In 2005, the total value of Alaska forest products was approximately $149 million (Halbrook et al. 2009). The bulk of the exported material was in log form, and total value of products exported to Asia was approximately $112 million, about 75 percent of the total value. Alaska's vast forest resources and proximity to Asia give the state a natural competitive advantage in supplying Asia with forest products.

Asia is the largest market for forest products exports from Alaska.

Asia is the largest market for forest products exports from Alaska. Japan is the largest Asian forest products market by imports and places a high value on Alaska wood's tight vertical grain properties (Roos et al. 2008b). However, as with the other global industries, Japan's forest products industry was heavily affected by the recent financial crisis. The major driver for Japan's forest products demand is housing starts, which declined 28 percent between 2008 and 2009 (JAWIC 2009). Although Japan will continue to be a strong market, future growth in Asian markets is expected to come from other Asian countries. Since the late 1990s, China and South Korea have experienced strong growth in their forest products markets. In 2009, the value of wood products (harmonized code 4400)[1] imported by these countries was US$6.5 billion for Japan, US$5.1 billion for China, and US$1.4 billion for South Korea (GTI 2009).

Why Export?

There are two major advantages of exporting. The first is revenue growth for forest products companies. Exporting requires a strong commitment from companies that includes adapting products to meet the needs of foreign markets, translating printed materials, developing relationships with foreign buyers, training personnel to understand foreign markets, and providing after-sale support for foreign customers. Exporters that invest the most effort in global markets are often the companies that thrive after economic downturns in these markets (Cunningham and Eastin 2002).

---

[1] Harmonized code is a multipurpose goods nomenclature used as the basis for Customs Tariffs and compilation trade statistics. The system was originally proposed by the U.N. World Customs Organization and implemented by an international convention on January 1, 1988. Additional information is available at the following Web sites: http://unstats. un.org/unsd/statcom/doc99/wcopaper.pdf; http://www.usitc.gov/tata/hts/index htm.

The second major advantage is market diversification. and ocean shipping is an essential component for attaining this advantage. Although the U.S. economy is still suffering. the Asian economies. led by China. are helping to lead the world out of the global recession. However. to supply the Asian markets. forest products companies need to understand and utilize ocean shipping. The purpose of this paper is to analyze recent trends in ocean shipping and their impact on Alaska forest products exporters.

Exchange Rates

One major factor influencing the shipping of U.S. forest products to global markets is exchange rates. Three major Asian currencies affecting Alaska's forest products are the Chinese yuan. the South Korean won. and the Japanese yen. Recently. the U.S. dollar has been losing value against these currencies making U.S. forest products more price competitive in the Asian markets. As of November 2010. 1 U.S. dollar is trading at approximately 81 Japanese yen. 1.107 South Korean won. and 6.65 Chinese yuan (Federal Reserve Bank 2010). Figure 1 compares the value of the currencies. using January 3. 2000. as a base year index in which all exchange values equal one. In this project. we are primarily concerned with Asian markets. but the value of the Euro has been included in figure 1 for reference purposes.

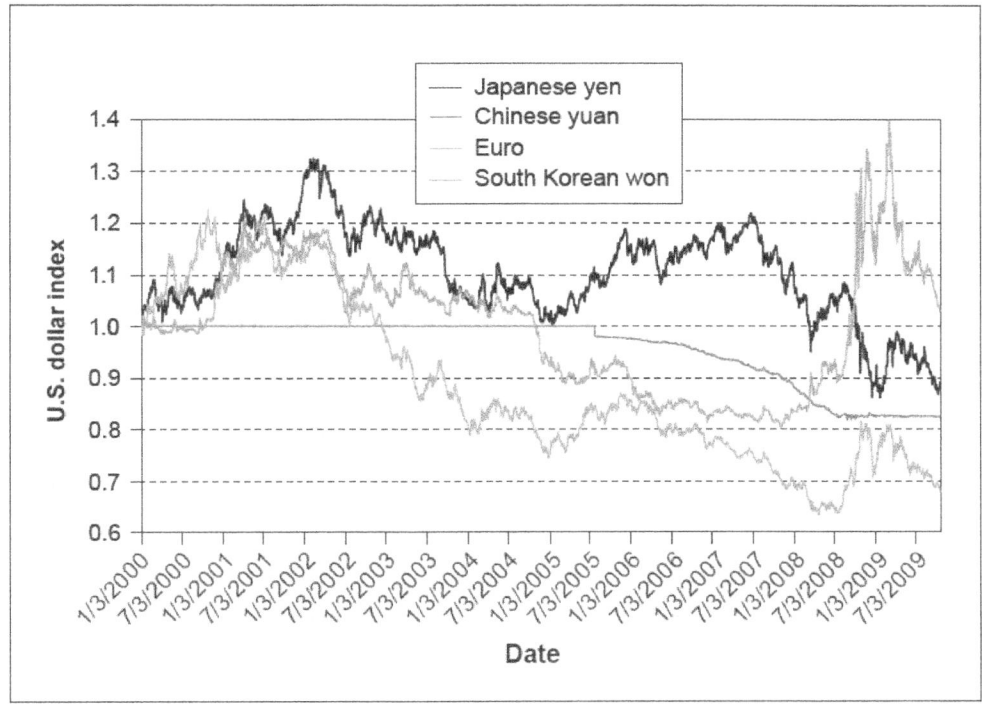

Figure 1—U.S. dollar indexed exchange rates (Index January 3. 2000 = 1).

Japan has the third largest economy in the world and the yen is a major global currency. Traditionally, the Bank of Japan has favored extremely low interest rates making the yen very attractive to global investors. Global investors will borrow yen at low interest rates, convert the yen to other currencies, and invest the funds where returns are higher. The funds are then converted back to yen once investment gains are realized and the yen-based loans are repaid. This global investment strategy is called the "yen carry trade" and has fueled demand for the yen. Between mid-2007 and 2010, the Japanese yen has increased substantially in value against the U.S. dollar.

In addition to the Japanese yen, the value of the South Korean won has also strengthened substantially against the U.S. dollar. The strength of the South Korean won can partially be attributed to South Korea's strong economic recovery. In the third quarter of 2009, South Korea's gross domestic product (GDP) annualized growth rate was 2.9 percent, the countries' highest growth rate in 7 years. Additionally, this was the third quarter of consecutive growth, showing that South Korea's recovery is on a sustainable path (Reuters 2009). In 2009, as South Korea's GDP growth improved, the won strengthened approximately 20 percent against the U.S. dollar from January to October. Furthermore, the median analyst forecast predicted the South Korean won would strengthen 7.4 percent further against the U.S. dollar by September 2010 (Brown and Lui 2009). The combination of an extremely cheap dollar against the won and a well-developed forest products market makes South Korea an important market for Alaska companies to examine.

In contrast to the Japanese yen and the South Korean won, the Chinese yuan is not a free-floating currency and thus currency swings are not as drastic.

In contrast to the Japanese yen and the South Korean won, the Chinese yuan is not a free-floating currency and thus currency swings are not as drastic. In 1994, inflation in China rose above 20 percent and the Chinese government implemented an economic stabilization plan. The pillar of this plan was to peg the Chinese yuan to the U.S. dollar at a rate of 8.28 yuan to 1 U.S. dollar. However, pressure mounted from China's trading partners to allow the yuan to float freely in the hope that the yuan would appreciate and reduce their mounting Chinese trade deficits. As a result, on July 21, 2005, the Chinese government initiated a managed float system against a basket of currencies. This system allowed the yuan to trade against a basket of currencies within a managed band. The basket of currencies includes the U.S. dollar, Euro, Japanese yen, South Korean won, and the British pound sterling. As of October 2010, the yuan has appreciated approximately 19.5 percent against the U.S. dollar since the managed float system was enacted. However, China has put the brakes on the yuan appreciation in reaction to the global economic crisis. The yuan has appreciated to 6.65 yuan to 1 U.S. dollar and is expected to remain at this level in order to help Chinese exporters weather the global recession (Brown and Lui 2009).

The future of the U.S. dollar remains uncertain. In 2009, the U.S. dollar softened against major currencies, making U.S. products more competitive abroad (fig. 1). Looking to the future, Brazil, India, China, and Russia have publicly announced their intentions to increase their non-U.S. dollar holdings in order to diversify their foreign reserves (Nozawa 2009). This, combined with the U.S. fiscal and trade deficits and inflation fears, will place more pressure on the U.S. dollar to depreciate further against major currencies.

Exportable Alaska Forest Products

The three major species that Alaska exports to Asia are Sitka spruce (*Picea sitchensis* (Bong.) Carrière), western hemlock (*Tsuga heterophylla* (Raf.) Sarg.), and Alaska yellow-cedar (*Chamaecyparis nootkatensis* (D. Don) Spach). One bright spot for the forest products industry since 2007 has been exports to Asia (Roos et al. 2008b). In contrast to domestic demand, which has fallen sharply since late 2007, demand for U.S. forest products in Asia has held fairly steady or actually increased. As described above, the largest forest products market in Asia is Japan, with China being a close second. The following sections examine the export volumes for logs and lumber of Alaska's three primary export species.

Sitka Spruce

Sitka spruce's primary end market in Asia is Japan. Most of the logs exported to China are milled into products that are re-exported to Japan and other developed nations. Japan values the light color of Sitka spruce for interior millwork including door and window trims, paneling, and shoji screen door frames.

Sitka spruce logs are categorized within trade statistics as spruce (*Picea* spp.), logs and timber, in the rough, not treated (harmonized code 4403200035). Total exports in this category have been increasing since 2000 (fig. 2). Canada is included in this section because it is the largest importer of U.S. spruce logs. The major Asian spruce log markets are China, Japan, and South Korea. Since 2000, Japan's spruce imports have declined by about 50 percent, whereas China's import volumes have surged by a factor of 13. It appears that China will surpass Japan in 2009 as the largest importer of U.S. spruce logs.

The second category examined was Sitka spruce lumber, which is categorized in the U.S. Customs statistics as Sitka spruce wood sawn (harmonized code 4407100017 and 18). The primary markets for Sitka spruce lumber in order of quantity are Japan, China, and Canada. In contrast to spruce logs, Sitka spruce lumber exports have declined dramatically since 2000 (fig. 3). For example, in 2000, Japan imported 66 859 m^3 (28,348 mbf) of Sitka spruce lumber and the volume for

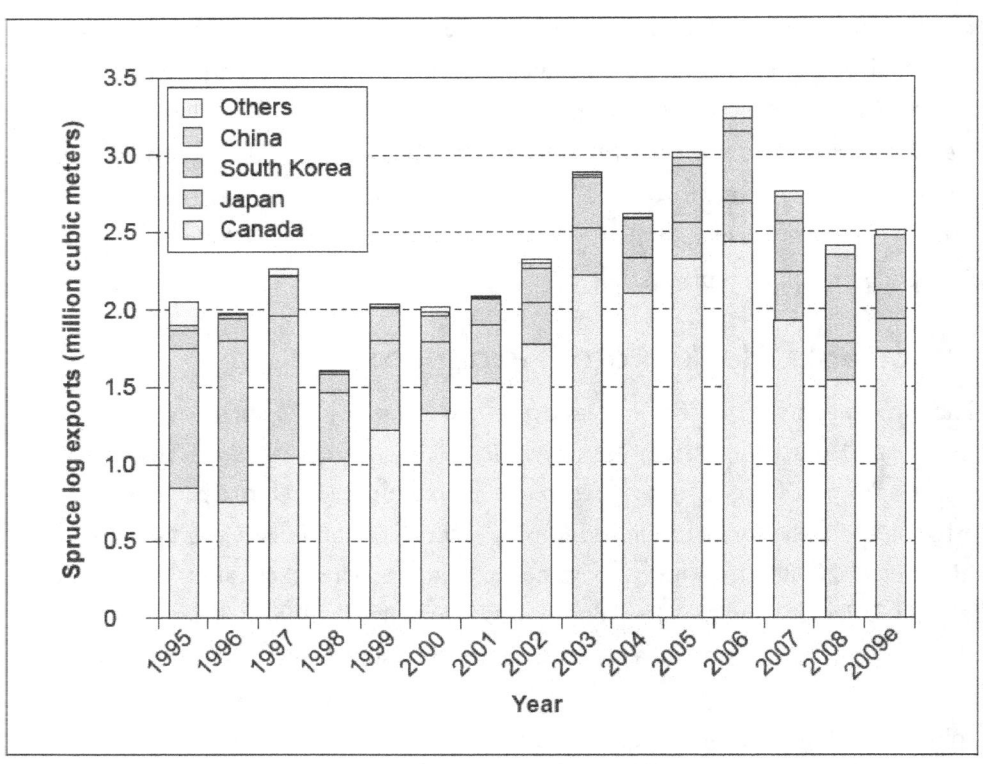

Figure 2—Spruce (*Picea* spp.) log exports from the United States (USITC 2009); e = estimate.

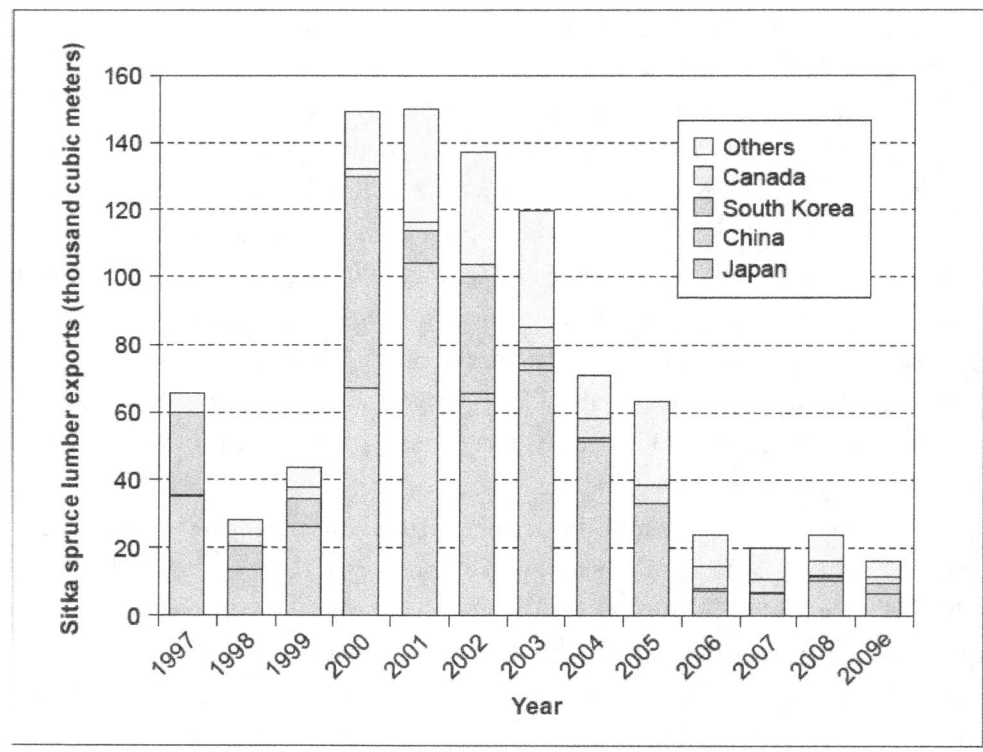

Figure 3—Sitka spruce lumber exports from the United States (USITC 2009); e = estimate.

2009 is projected to be approximately 6271 m^3 (2,659 mbf). The major cause for the decline in the Sitka spruce lumber category has been the shift in Japan from importing lumber directly from North America to utilizing more European white-wood (mainly *Picea abies* (L.) Karst.) and importing spruce lumber milled in China from imported logs. Japan is followed by China and Canada, which are projected to import 2917 and 1861 m^3 (1,236 and 789 mbf) of Sitka spruce lumber, respectively.

Alaska Hemlock

Both western hemlock and mountain hemlock (*Tsuga mertensiana* (Bong.) Carrière) grow in Alaska. In the extreme northern areas of southeast Alaska, harvested material may include both species (Harlow and Harrar 1958). In the southern areas of the region, harvested areas support stands of western hemlock. The characteristics that distinguish western hemlock from mountain hemlock are needle, cone, and location-based characteristics. In the sawn form, mountain hemlock is more dense, but it is impossible to visually identify the species of origin. In the past, the primary use of exported hemlock was for Japan baby squares or posts used in traditional Japanese post and beam construction. However, starting in the mid-1990s, the Japanese market shifted to use of European whitewood lumber and laminated posts, and hemlock exports declined rapidly. Recently, demand for hemlock has increased as the U.S. dollar has depreciated against other major currencies.

Hemlock logs are categorized in the U.S. Customs data as western hemlock logs and timber (harmonized code 4403200050). The U.S. Custom data show that in 2009, the United States exported approximately 625 000 m^3 (138,889 mbf) of western hemlock logs to South Korea, almost double the volume of 2000 (fig. 4). South Korea is increasing its use of western hemlock for construction applications, crating, and packaging materials (Roos et al. 2009). This country has blossomed as a value-added manufacturing hub that produces high-quality cars, high-end electronics, and heavy industry; which has fueled demand for crating, dunnage, and packaging. China and Japan also import western hemlock logs and their projected 2009 volumes are 83 500 m^3 (18,555 mbf) and 27 000 m^3 (6,000 mbf), respectively.

Western hemlock lumber is categorized in the trade data as hemlock wood sawn (code 4407100064 and 65). In 2009, the top three Asian markets for western hemlock lumber are projected to be China with about 37 000 m^3 (15,688 mbf) Japan with about 16 000 m^3 (6,784 mbf), and South Korea with about 3600 m^3 (1,524 mbf) (fig. 5) (GTI 2009). Canada was included in this analysis for comparison purposes because it is the largest hemlock lumber export market for the United States, with 2009 volumes expected to reach 49 000 m^3 (20,776 mbf).

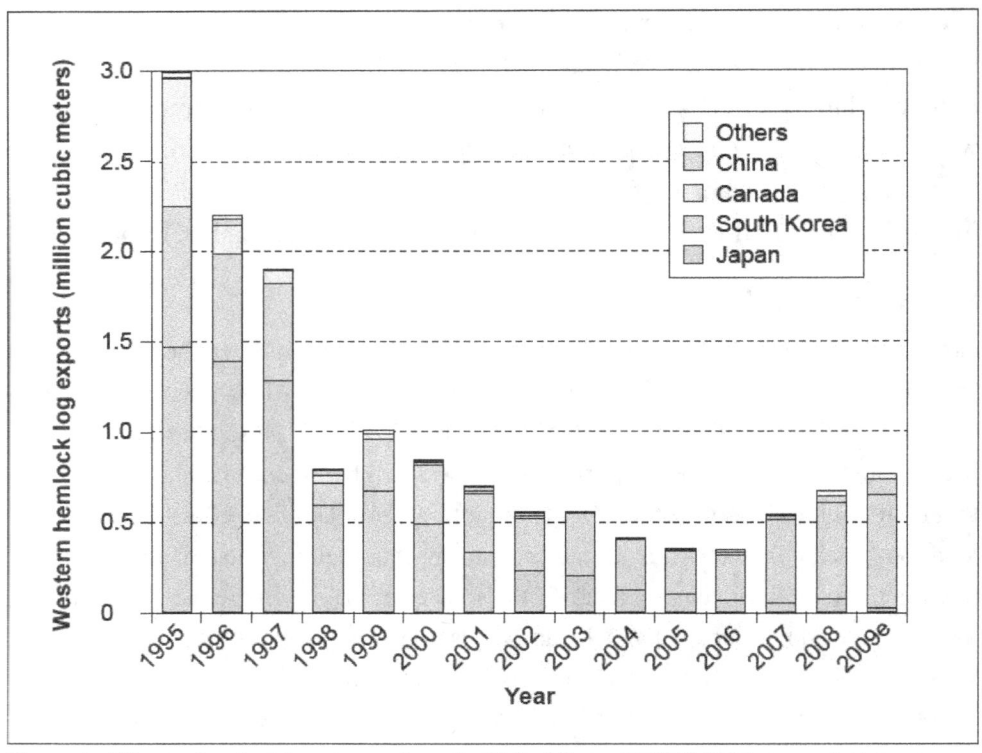

Figure 4—Western hemlock log exports from the United States (USITC 2009); e = estimate.

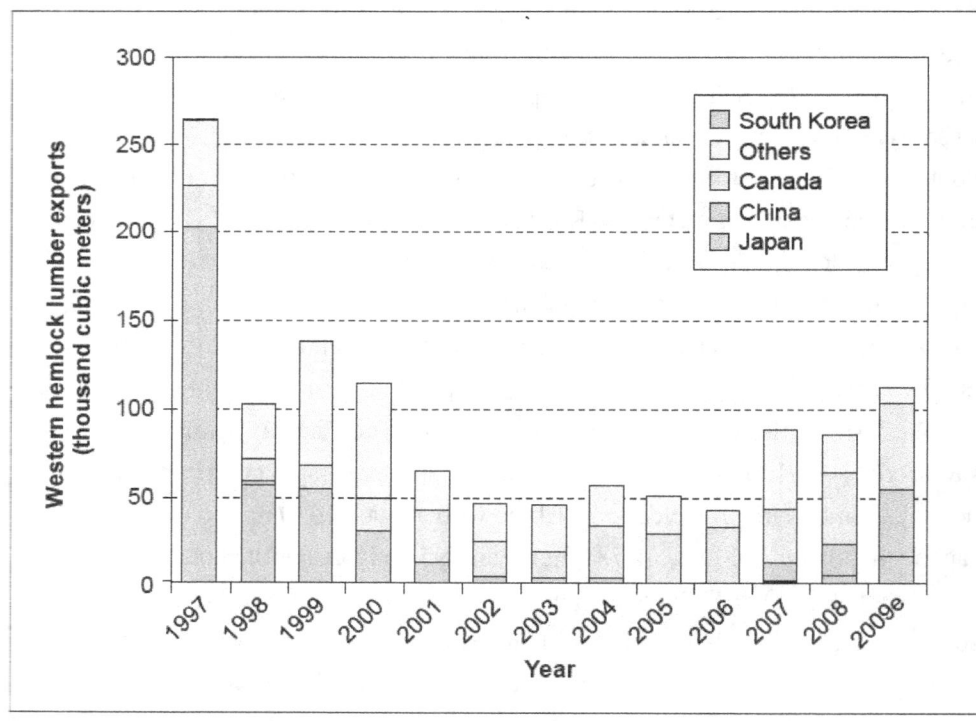

Figure 5—Western hemlock lumber exports from the United States (USITC 2009); e = estimate.
Note: South Korea included in "Others" for the years 1988–2009.

Alaska Yellow-Cedar

Owing to its natural decay-resistant properties, Japan uses Alaska yellow-cedar (*Chamaecyparis nootkatensis* (D. Don) Spach) for sill plates (dodai) in their traditional post and beam construction. The sill plates lie on top of the cement foundation between the foundation and the wood frame of the house. Alaska yellow-cedar is also used for lamstock to manufacture glulam beams for exterior applications. Although this species is fairly popular in Japan, a majority of Alaska yellow-cedar is imported from Canada rather than the United States. The U.S. Customs data do not track Alaska yellow-cedar log exports as a separate category. However, Japan imports can be tracked through the Japanese government customs data (Japan Customs Bureau 2009). It is projected that in 2009 the United States will export approximately 18 000 m^3 (3,996 mbf) of Alaska yellow-cedar logs to Japan, and Canada will export approximately 22 000 m^3 (4,884 mbf) (GTI 2009). Alaska yellow-cedar log exports to China must be estimated from the "other" coniferous log category (code 4403200060) in the U.S. International Trade Commission data (USITC 2009). For 2009, Alaska yellow-cedar log exports to China are projected to be 4000 m^3 (888 mbf), which is roughly 10 percent of the volume in the "other" log category described above.

Alaska yellow-cedar lumber is categorized within the U.S. International Trade Commission data as yellow cedar sawn (code 4407100074 and 75). Alaska yellow-cedar lumber exports from the United States are relatively small with total exports slightly over 2000 m^3 (848 mbf) in 2009 (fig. 6). In contrast, it is projected that Canada will export approximately 80 000 m^3 (33,920 mbf) of Alaska yellow-cedar lumber to Japan in 2009 (Japan Customs Bureau 2009).

In examining the above data on all three species, it is important to note that many of the finished products from the logs exported to China end up in Japan. Alaska forest products can enter Japan via various distribution channels including exporting logs and lumber directly to Japan, or exporting logs to China, where they are milled and exported to Japan as lumber or other value-added forest products. The first two channels are easy to track via trade statistics. However, lumber that ends up in Japan via logs exported to China is more difficult to track. In fall 2008, a research project was undertaken to address the question of how logs exported from Alaska to China are being utilized. The researchers visited importers of Alaska logs in China and conducted interviews on how the logs were used and where the finished products were being distributed. The results showed that a majority of the clear portion of the logs were milled and exported to Japan directly or manufactured into other products such as glulam beams, millwork, and furniture, and then exported to Japan (Roos et al. 2009). The clear lumber is cut out of the log, and the cut stock is efficiently used

Many of the finished products from the logs exported to China end up in Japan.

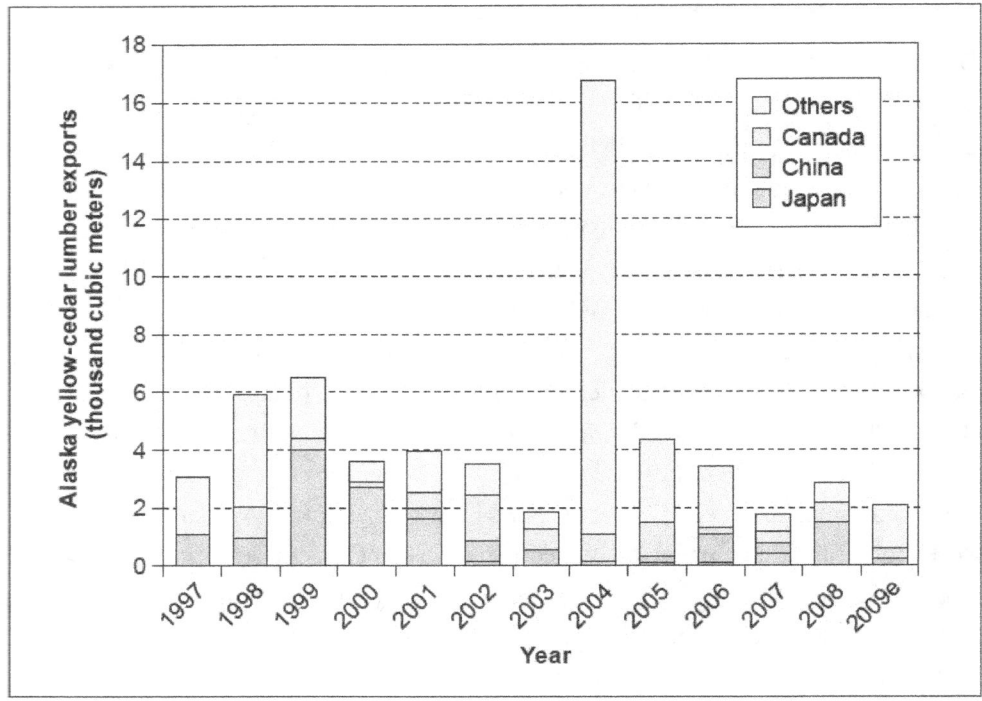

Figure 6—Alaska yellow-cedar lumber exports from the United States (USITC 2009); e = estimate.

for a variety of applications including laminated boards, door cores, and furniture. In conclusion, the weakening of the U.S. dollar makes Alaska forest products very attractive in Asia, which provides an opportunity for Alaska mills to increase their revenue.

Other Species

Two other species that are indigenous to southeast Alaska are noted. Limited amounts of western red cedar (*Thuja plicata* Donn ex D. Don) are exported in log form. Logs of this species from old trees commonly are hollow butted and have extensive amounts of pecky heart rot (Harlow and Harrar 1958). Given a low ratio of recoverable material in relation to shipping weight, much of this material is sawn by local mills into products such as decking, siding, fencing, and shingles. Much of the red cedar product produced in the region is sold to local and national markets.

Many of the areas cut during the last 50 years, especially areas with heavy soil disturbance, have regenerated to stands of red alder (*Alnus rubra* Bong.). The oldest of these stands is now approaching maturity. Recent research (Brackley et al. 2009) indicates that the grade recovery from logs of this species is comparable to material from other regions of the Pacific Northwest. Little of this material is now being harvested, but in the future, it may be an exportable product in either log or lumber form.

Global Shipping Trends

Global shipping made significant leaps in the latter half of the 20th century. Some of the most significant developments have been cargo containerization, intermodal transport, the increased role of non vessel operating common carriers (NVOCCs) and freight forwarders, and shipping deregulation resulting from the Shipping Act of 1984 and the Ocean Shipping Reform Act of 1998.

Containerization is the shipping of freight in standardized 20- and 40-foot shipping containers. Before containerization, a majority of freight was shipped as break bulk cargo. This made loading, unloading, and transferring of cargo to different modes of transportation extremely labor intensive. One of the first companies to attack these inefficiencies was Alaska Steamship,[2] which started using metal shipping boxes in 1949 (Kendall and Buckley 2001).

Another major development in the shipping industry was the increase in intermodal transportation, defined as a systems approach in which goods are moved in a continuous movement from origin to destination using two or more modes of transportation (Kendall and Buckley 2001). During the transport from origin to destination, the container is not opened and the freight itself is not handled. For example, a 40-foot container of freight going from Chicago to Asia may travel by rail, truck, and ocean carrier. The container is transferred seamlessly from one mode of transportation to the next without being opened and the freight being handled. Intermodal transport allowed containerization to flourish by integrating the various modes of transportation including trucking, rail, ocean, and air into a fast and efficient transportation system.

The third development in shipping was the increased role for freight forwarders and NVOCCs. Intermodal transportation requires firms that specialize in coordinating the various modes of transportation into seamless point-to-point shipments, a role filled by NVOCCs and freight forwarders. An NVOCC is a common carrier that coordinates transportation and issues its own ocean bills of lading or other equivalent documents, but does not operate the vessels by which ocean transportation is provided. It also serves the role of consolidating shipments from various shippers. A freight forwarder is a third-party logistics agent that coordinates shipments for its customers. Freight forwarding services include booking cargo, preparing shipping and export documentation, consolidating freight, obtaining cargo insurance, and filing insurance claims. Many of the roles of freight forwarders and NVOCCs overlap. However, the difference between a freight forwarder and

---

[2] The use of trade or firm names in this publication is for reader information and does not imply endorsement by the U.S. Department of Agriculture of any product or service.

an NVOCC is that a freight forwarder acts as an agent for the shipper, whereas an NVOCC is a legally defined shipper and not an agent. Both NVOCCs and freight forwarders are licensed by the Federal Maritime Commission, and many freight forwarders also have a NVOCC license.

Another major development was increased deregulation in the ocean shipping industry through legislation. One of the roles of the Federal Maritime Commission is to regulate agreements among groups of ocean carriers called conferences. Conferences are agreements between two or more shipping companies to provide scheduled cargo service on a particular trade route under uniform rates. These agreements also regulate the ocean shipping capacity of the trade routes their members serve. The major conferences with carriers serving the U.S. west coast/Asia trade routes are the New World Alliance, the Grand Alliance, and the CKYH Alliance. The New World Alliance includes the American President Lines (APL), Hyundai Merchant Marine (HMM), and Mitsui OSK Lines (MOL). The Grand Alliance includes Hapag-Lloyd, MISC Berhad, Nippon Yusen Kaisha (NYK), and the Orient Overseas Container Line (OOCL). The CKYH Alliance includes China Ocean Shipping Company (COSCO), Kawasaki Kisen Kaisha (K-Line), Yang Ming Marine Transport, and Hanjin Shipping Company. Inherently, agreements among competing firms that set prices and limit capacity are in violation of U.S. antitrust laws. However, ocean shipping carrier conferences are allowed to set rates and control capacity within the United States because the Shipping Act of 1916 provides ocean shipping carrier conferences with immunity from U.S antitrust laws.

In 1978, transportation deregulation was set in motion with the Airline Deregulation Act. One of the goals of this legislation was to increase competition among the airlines by removing government regulation of fares, routes, and schedules. This environment of deregulation led to an effort to stimulate more competition in the ocean shipping industry and reduce the power of ocean shipping conferences. The Shipping Act of 1984 was enacted to increase competition in the ocean shipping industry (Donovan and Bonney 2006). This act, while maintaining the antitrust immunity, required that conference agreements allow any carrier wishing to serve a specific trade route be admitted to the conference and any member wishing to leave the conference be allowed to leave the conference. It also increased market forces by allowing any conference member to take any independent action on rates. The expansion of market forces increased further with the Ocean Shipping Reform Act (OSRA) of 1998. This act required that members of conference agreements also be allowed to sign confidential contracts with shippers without violating the conference agreements. The major impact of OSRA was to increase the number of private shipping contracts between companies that ship products and ocean carriers. For example, a retail chain importing a large volume from China could negotiate rates directly with an ocean carrier and these rates may be lower than the conference agreement rates. The Ocean Shipping Reform Act of 1998 resulted in a surge of private shipper/carrier contracts. The year following OSRA, the Federal Maritime Commission received 116 percent more applications for private shipper/carrier contracts than the previous year (Creel 2000). The rates established by private shipper/carrier agreements often were more favorable than rates set by conference agreements, thereby reducing the importance of conference agreements. This act also increased efficiencies for intermodal transportation by permitting ocean carriers to offer inland transportation (Kendell and Buckley 2001).

Ocean Shipping Rates and Volumes

The most recent event to affect the ocean shipping industry was the global economic crisis, which began with the U.S. mortgage crisis in late 2007. The slowdown in the global economy has led to excess shipping capacity and a decline in rates. Port traffic and ship container capacity are measured in 20-foot equivalent units (TEUs), which is the number of standard 20-foot containers that a port handles annually or that can fit on a container ship. For example, one standard 20-foot container equals one TEU, and one standard 40-foot container equals two TEUs. Figure 7 shows a sudden decline in 2008 in the volume of North American shipping activity as measured in TEUs handled by ports in the United States, Canada, and Mexico. The volumes declined further in 2009, leading to a glut of capacity. Many

Container capacity is measured in 20-foot equivalent units (TEUs), which is the number of standard 20-foot containers that a port handles annually.

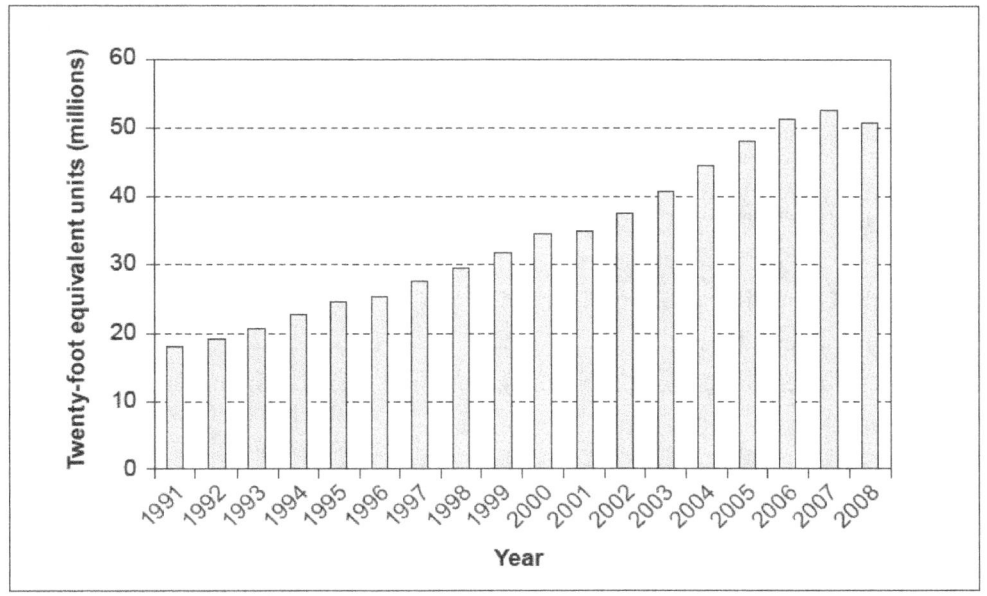

Figure 7—North American (United States, Mexico, and Canada) shipping volumes in 20-foot equivalent units (AAPA 2009).

container ships are sitting idle in Singapore, where ships are often stored when they are not needed. At the same time, new ships ordered before the global credit crisis are nearing completion and will further increase the glut of capacity (Forsyth 2009).

There are two methods for shipping Alaska forest products to Asia. The first is chartered ocean vessel and the second is a container ship with scheduled ports of call. Generally, charter vessels are used to transport raw materials such as oil, grain, coal, steel scrap, and logs. The advantage of a chartered vessel is flexibility in specifying cargo loading, offloading ports, and shipping dates. Traditionally, log exporters have employed specialty log charter ships. However, if log export charter ships are not available or too costly, logs can be cut to fit in standard sized 40-foot or high cube 40-foot containers. Given the availability of containers being returned to Asian countries, increasing volumes of logs are being shipped by this method.

In contrast to chartering a vessel, shipping in a standardized shipping container via a scheduled ocean carrier service is generally cheaper than chartering for bulk cargo. Lumber is normally shipped either in a 20- or 40-foot standardized shipping container. The weight and dimension specifications of standardized shipping containers are shown in table 1. The weight of the lumber differs depending on whether it is green or kiln dried. The advantage of shipping kiln-dried lumber is that you reduce the water weight of the product, which also reduces the shipping costs.

Table 1—Standard shipping container sizes

	Inside length	Inside width	Inside height	Door width	Door height	Capacity	Tare weight	Maximum cargo
	---------------- Feet ----------------					Cubic feet	- - - - Pounds - - - -	
Standard 20 foot	19.33	7.67	7.83	7.67	7.5	1,172	4,916	47,900
Standard 40 foot	39.42	7.67	7.83	7.67	7.5	2,390	8,160	59,040

Source: SR International Logistics 2010.

Depending on the density of the cargo, the limiting factor will be either the weight of the cargo or the cubic dimensions of the cargo. For example, a low-density cargo will reach the cubic volume limitations of a container before it reaches the weight restrictions of the container. Table 2 shows various commodities, their density, and how they compare to lumber. In contrast to a lower density cargo, a fairly dense cargo such as lumber will reach the weight restrictions of a container before exceeding the cubic-volume restrictions.

Table 2—Density of various commodities

Commodity	Density
	Pounds per cubic foot
Douglas-fir lumber	35
Baled hay or straw	8–14
Feed grains	32
Ear corn	28
Potatoes	43
Fruits and vegetables	30–40

Source: Carson 1989.

Another important constraint when shipping lumber in containers is road weight restrictions. The Federal Highway Administration has a formula for weight restrictions based on the gross vehicle weight including tractor, number of trailer axles, and the space between the axles. For example, a trailer with three axles where the first and third axles are spaced 97 inches apart can carry a load of 42,000 pounds (U.S. Department of Transportation FHA 2009). Thus, although the container has the capacity to carry 59,040 pounds of cargo, the freight, if moved over the highway system is limited by the Federal Highway Administration weight restrictions. Foreign countries also have similar road weight restrictions, and these need to be checked if the cargo is going to travel inland from the foreign port.

The general rate movement of bulk cargo is tracked by the Baltic Exchange. The Baltic Exchange is an intermediary exchange that brings together ship brokers, ship owners, and charterers to buy and sell bulk commodity shipping space in the global market. The Baltic Dry Index (BDI) is an index based on the average shipping prices for dry bulk cargo on the Baltic Exchange. The index shows how ocean shipping prices peaked in mid-2008, and then declined sharply in the beginning of 2009 (Bloomberg 2010). Another factor influencing Asia-bound shipping container prices is the U.S. trade deficit, which has caused a glut of empty Asia-bound containers to be located on the west coast. The United States imports a large quantity of goods from Asia and exports a smaller quantity. For example, in Washington State, the export/import ratio is approximately 72 percent; in Oregon, it is approximately 98 percent, and at the Port of Vancouver (British Columbia), it is 72 percent (Goodchild et al. 2008).

Developing a historical time series of container rates for lumber is made more difficult because there is no general index such as the BDI for lumber container rates. The Federal Maritime Commission requires that carriers file their tariffs or rates by commodity class with the Federal Maritime Commission (Federal Maritime Commission 2009). However, forest products are exempt from this requirement, making it very difficult to track ocean carrier container rates for lumber. For the purpose of this research, the Pacific Northwest Asia Shippers Association provided the researchers with estimates of lumber ocean shipping rates based on their negotiated contracts. Ocean shipping companies often add additional charges to their shipping rates including bunker adjustment factors (BAF) to accommodate for fluctuations in fuel prices and currency adjustment factor to adjust for currency fluctuations. For example, in April 2009, the rate for a 40-foot container from Oakland to Tokyo for almonds was $1,400 plus a $226 BAF plus a $40 transfer charge, for a total rate of $1,666 (USDA AMS 2009). Figure 8 shows the approximate annual rates for a 40-foot container of lumber from Seattle to Tokyo, including BAF. These rates fluctuated from $680 to $1,325 between 1997 and 2009. As of November 2009, the lumber rate is approximately $800 per 40-foot container.

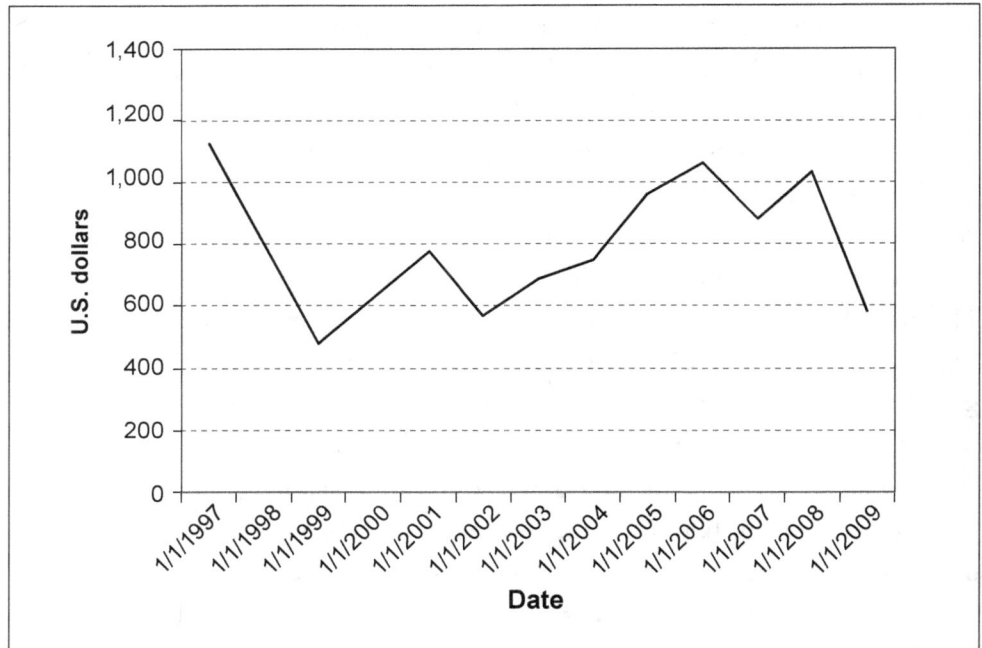

Figure 8—Estimated lumber ocean shipping rates from Seattle to Tokyo per 40-foot container (PNASA 2009).

In addition to lumber rates, ocean shipping rates for soy, almonds, and hay were examined. The U.S. Department of Agriculture, Agricultural Transportation Division publishes these statistics quarterly, and the annual rates for April were compared to lumber. It is important to note that the soy, almond, and hay rates are tariff rates and do not necessarily reflect actual shipping rates that are negotiated between companies and the ocean carriers. As discussed above, lumber rates are exempt from the Federal Maritime Commission's tariff publishing requirements and therefore rates negotiated privately by an association were used. The analysis below compares lumber rates to rates for almonds, soy, and hay. It is important to note that the published shipping rates for almonds, soy, and hay may be higher than the actual rates that shippers negotiate with ocean carriers. Therefore, the data are used to present approximate costs to ship products from the Port of Seattle to the Port of Tokyo and to correlate various rates to lumber shipping rates.

An analysis was conducted to examine the relationship between the lumber rates and other commodity rates. From 2001 to 2009, the mean shipping cost was $1,690 for almonds, $1,563 for soybeans, $1,347 for hay, and $1,014 for lumber (table 3). The researchers used SPSS statistical software to conduct a Pearson correlation and ordinary least squares regression. The results of the Pearson correlation showed that lumber rates are most closely correlated to hay. The correlation between lumber and hay is significant with a correlation coefficient of 0.72 (table 4). The correlation coefficient for hay was followed by almonds with a coefficient of 0.65 and soybeans with a coefficient of -0.37. The researchers also examined the relationship between oil prices and ocean shipping rates. There was a statistically significant relationship between oil and both hay and lumber shipping rates. Fuel is a large part of the cost of ocean shipping, and as oil prices rise, shipping rates also tend to rise.

Lumber rates are most closely correlated to hay.

Table 3—Ocean shipping rates from Seattle to Tokyo for 40-foot containers

Year	Almonds	Soybeans	Hay	Lumber
		Dollars		
2001	1,555	1,760	1,337	980
2002	1,170	1,520	929	770
2003	1,897	1,926	1,015	890
2004	1,350	1,147	746	950
2005	2,014	1,436	1,737	1,165
2006	2,151	1,099	1,510	1,265
2007	1,258	1,789	1,539	1,085
2008	2,153	1,643	1,915	1,235
2009	1,666	1,745	1,394	783
Mean	1,690	1,563	1,347	1,014

Source: USDA AMS 2009.

Table 4—Pearson Correlation and Regression results for ocean shipping rates

	Soybean rates	Almond rates	Hay rates	Lumber rates
Correlation coefficient to lumber rates	-0.37	0.65	0.72^a	1
Correlation coefficient to oil prices	-0.07	0.49	0.78^a	0.69^a
R-squared (dependent variable = lumber rates)	0.14	0.43	0.52^a	Dependent variable

[a] Significant at the 0.05 level.

As a followup to the correlation analysis, three ordinary least squares linear regression equations were run using lumber shipping rates as the dependent variable and each of the respective commodity shipping rates as the independent variable. The results showed that hay was the only significant predictor for lumber shipping rates, with a coefficient of 0.35 and an R-squared value of 0.52. Therefore, even though there are no published rates for lumber, organizations can use the published rates for hay to get a rough idea for the shipping cost. Rates for hay and other commodities can be found at the USDA Agricultural Marketing Service (2009) Web site that is listed in the appendix.

Ports

The main ports with container terminal capability that serve southeast Alaska forest products Asian exports are the Port of Seattle and the Port of Tacoma. Selected port schedules showing carriers, carrier alliances, and trade routes are shown in tables 5, 6, and 7. The schedules are constantly changing, and these tables were included as a general reference rather than an exact shipping schedule. The one Alaska barge line

Table 5—Port of Tacoma selected shipping schedules by carrier

Primary carrier	ETA	ETD	Alliance	Partner carriers	Port rotation schedule
Evergreen (1ˢᵗ route)	Fri	Sat	NA	NA	Tacoma, Taipei, Kaohsiung, Yantian, Hong Kong, Kaohsiung, Los Angeles, Oakland, Tacoma
Evergreen (2ⁿᵈ route)	Fri	Sat	NA	NA	Tacoma, Vancouver , Tokyo, Osaka, Qingdao, Shanghai, Ningbo, Taipei, Kaohsiung, Hong Kong, Yantian, Tanjung Pelepas, Colombo, Ashdod, Dekheila, Taranto, Genoa, Barcelona, Valencia, Taranto, Port Said, Colombo, Tanjung Pelepas, Kaohsiung, Yantian, Hong Kong, Taipei, Osaka, Tokyo, Tacoma
Hyundai Merchant Marine	Mon or Fri	Tues or Sat	New World Alliance	APL, MOL	Tacoma, Seattle, Vancouver, Tacoma, Busan, Kwangyang, Kaohsiung, Hong Kong, Yantian, Shanghai, Busan, Tokyo, Tacoma
Kawasaki Kisen Kaisha	Sat	Sun	CKYH Alliance	COSCO, Hanjin, Yang Ming	Tacoma, Vancouver, Kobe, Tokyo, Nagoya, Kaohsiung, Xiamen, Hong Kong, Yantian, Shanghai, Nagoya, Tokyo, Tacoma
Mitsui OSK Lines	Wed	Thurs	New World Alliance	APL, HMM	Tacoma, Vancouver, Tokyo, Osaka, Kobe, Nagoya, Shimizu, Tokyo, Los Angeles, Oakland, Tacoma
Yang Ming Transport	Sat	Sun	CKYH Alliance	COSCO, Hanjin, "K" Line	Tacoma, Los Angeles, Oakland, Pusan, Kwangyang, Shanghai, Ningbo, Pusan, Tacoma
Horizon Barge Lines	Wed Fri Sun	Wed Fri Sun	NA	NA	Tacoma, Anchorage, Kodiak, Tacoma, Anchorage, Kodiak, Dutch Harbor, Tacoma

ETA = estimated time of arrival; ETD = estimated time of departure, NA = not applicable.
APL = American President Lines; COSCO = China Ocean Shipping Company; Hanjin = Hanjin Shipping Company; HMM = Hyundai Merchant Marine; "K" Line = Kawasaki; MOL = Mitsui OSK Lines; Yang Ming = Yang Ming Marine Transport; CKYH Alliance =COSCO, "K" Line, Yang Ming, and Hanjin; New World Alliance = APL, HMM, and MOL.
Source: Port of Tacoma 2009.

Table 6—Port of Seattle container ship sailing schedule outline

Primary carrier	ETA	ETD	Alliance	Partner carriers	Port rotation schedule
APL	Fri.	Sun.	New World Alliance	Hyundai, MOL	Seattle, Vancouver, Yokohama, Kobe, Kaohsiung, Chiwan, Laem Chabang, Singapore, Port Klang, Kaohsiung, Hong Kong, Yantian, Shanghai, Busan, Tokyo, Tacoma, Seattle
Westwood Shipping	Wed.	Thurs.	NA	NA	Seattle, Hitachinaka, Shimizu, Tokyo, Busan, Osaka, Nagoya, Shimuzu, Tokyo, Everett, Seattle
OOCL (1st route)	Mon.	Wed.	Grand Alliance	NYK, Hapag-Lloyd, MISC Berhad	Seattle, Vancouver, Tokyo, Nagoya, Kobe, Ningbo, Kaohsiung, Yantian, Hong Kong, Tokyo, Nagoya, Seattle
OOCL (2nd route)	Wed.	Fri.	Grand Alliance	NYK, Hapag-Lloyd, MISC Berhad	Seattle, Busan, Kaohsiung, Hong Kong, Shekou, Ningbo, Shanghai, Qingdao, Busan, Seattle
CSCL	Sun.	Mon.	NA	NA	Seattle, Vancouver, Nansha, Hong Kong, Yantian, Shanghai, Ningbo, Busan, Seattle
COSCO (1st route)	Sun.	Mon.	CKYH Alliance	Hanjin, Yang Ming, "K" Line	Seattle, Yokohama, Shanghai, Busan, Seattle
COSCO (2nd route)	Sun.	Mon.	CKYH Alliance	Hanjin, Yang Ming, "K" Line	Seattle, Vancouver, Nansha, Hong Kong, Yantian, Shanghai, Ningbo, Busan, Hong Kong, Yantian, Yokohama, Prince Rupert, Vancouver, Seattle
Northland Services, Inc.	Thurs.	Mon.	NA	NA	Seattle, Ketchikan, Petersburg, Juneau, Sitka, Wrangell, Thorne Bay, Metlakatla, Seattle

ETA = estimated time of arrival, EDT = estimated departure time; NA = not applicable.

APL = American President Lines; COSCO = China Ocean Shipping Company; CSCL = China Shipping Container Lines Co., Ltd.; Hanjin = Hanjin Shipping Company; Hapag-Lloyd = Hapag-Lloyd AG; HMM = Hyundai Merchant Marine; "K" Line = Kawasaki; MISC Berhad = Malaysia International Shipping Corporation Berhad; MOL = Mitsui OSK Lines; NYK = Nippon Yusen Kaisha; OOCL = Orient Overseas Container Line; Yang Ming = Yang Ming Marine Transport; CKYH Alliance = COSCO, "K" Line, Yang Ming, and Hanjin; Grand Alliance = Hapag-Lloyd, MISC Berhad, and OOCL; New World Alliance = APL, HMM, and MOL.

Source: Port of Seattle 2009.

Table 7—Example of Prince Rupert container ship sailing schedules

Primary carrier	ETA	ETD	Alliance	Partner carriers	Port rotation schedule
COSCO (1st route)	Wed.	Thurs.	CKYH Alliance	Hanjin, Yang Ming, "K" Line	Prince Rupert, Vancouver, Seattle, Yokohama, Shanghai, Hong Kong, Yantian, Yokohama, Prince Rupert
COSCO (2nd route)	Wed.	Thurs.	CKYH Alliance	Hanjin, Yang Ming, "K" Line	Prince Rupert, Long Beach, Oakland, Yokohama, Dalian, Xingang, Qingdao, Shanghai, Prince Rupert
Hanjin	Wed.	Thurs.	CKYH Alliance	COSCO, Yang Ming, "K" Line	Prince Rupert, Vancouver, Seattle, Yokohama, Shanghai, Busan, Hong Kong, Yantian, Yokohama, Prince Rupert

ETA = estimated time of arrival, ETD = estimated time of departure.

COSCO = China Ocean Shipping Company; Hanjin = Hanjin Shipping Company; "K" Line = Kawasaki; Yang Ming = Yang Ming Marine Transport; CKYH Alliance = COSCO, "K" Line, Yang Ming, and Hanjin.

Source: Prince Rupert Port Authority 2009.

Some barge lines serving Seattle do not allow their containers to go to Asia. Material in containers from these companies must be unloaded and transferred to a shipping container owned by an ocean carrier serving Asia.

that connects southeast Alaska to the Port of Seattle is Northland. This connection allows for intermodal service from southeast Alaska to Asia. A Northland container could be loaded in southeast Alaska and transshipped to a container ship at the Port of Seattle without unloading the cargo and having to transfer it to another container. Some other barge lines serving Seattle do not allow their containers to go to Asia. Thus, the barge line container must be unloaded and transferred to a shipping container owned by the ocean carrier that ships to Asia.

One major development in the North American global shipping industry has been the establishment of the Port of Prince Rupert (British Columbia) in 2007. During its first full year of operation in 2008, the Port of Prince Rupert moved 181,890 TEUs, which is a very small volume compared to other global ports. For example, in 2007, the number one port by volume was Singapore, which handled 27.9 million TEUs. On the west coast, the Port of Los Angeles handled about 8.35 million TEUs, and the Port of Seattle and the Port of Tacoma handled about 1.9 million TEUs each (table 8). These data show that the Port of Prince Rupert is relatively small on a global scale. However, the port has phase II expansion plans to quadruple its capacity to a total of 2 million TEUs. This phase would also extend the wharf 800 m (2,600 ft), reach an 18-m (59-ft) water depth, increase the dock area to 56 ha (139 acres), and increase storage capacity to 28,560 TEUs. It would also increase the number of post-panamax cranes from two to eight. These cranes are equipped with the latest technology and have the ability to load and unload larger container ships (Prince Rupert Port Authority 2009).

The development of the Port of Prince Rupert has significant potential for Alaska's forest products industry. Approximately 74 percent of Alaska's timber harvest in 2005 originated in southeast Alaska (Halbrook et al. 2009), and the Port of Prince Rupert opens up a new gateway to ship these products to Asia. The Port of Prince Rupert is significantly closer to southeast Alaska than are the ports of Seattle or the Tacoma. The distance from Ketchikan to Prince Rupert is about 85 mi, which is a sharp contrast to the 679 mi distance from Ketchikan to Seattle. Furthermore, the Port of Prince Rupert is 1 day closer to Asian ports than the Seattle and Tacoma ports. The critical missing link to connect southeast Alaska to the Port of Prince Rupert is a scheduled barge service.

Although the Port of Prince Rupert has potential as an Asian gateway for southeast Alaska, the essential component missing is scheduled barge service between southeast Alaska and Prince Rupert. The main companies with scheduled barge service between southeast Alaska and Seattle are Alaska Marine Lines, Boyer Barge, and Northland. As of this writing, none of these barge lines have service to Prince Rupert. However, the Canadian National Railroad (CN) runs a rail barge

Table 8—Port rankings by 20-foot equivalent units (TEUs)

Rank	Port	Country	TEUs
1	Singapore	Singapore	27,935,500
2	Shanghai	China	26,152,400
3	Hong Kong	China	23,998,449
4	Shenzhen	China	21,103,800
5	Yingkou (Liaonian)	China	13,713,000
6	Busan	South Korea	13,254,703
7	Rotterdam	Netherlands	10,790,604
8	Dubai Ports	UAE	10,653,026
9	Kaohsiung	Taiwan	10,256,829
10	Hamburg	Germany	9,917,180
11	Qingdao	China	9,430,600
12	Ningbo	China	9,258,800
13	Guangzhou	China	9,200,000
14	Los Angeles	USA	8,355,038
15	Antwerp	Belgium	8,175,951
16	Long Beach	USA	7,312,465
17	Port Kelang	Malaysia	7,118,714
18	Tianjin	China	7,102,100
19	Tanjung Pelepas	Malaysia	5,500,000
20	New York/New Jersey	USA	5,299,105
21	Bremen/Bremerhaven	Germany	4,892,056
22	Laem Chabang	Thailand	4,641,915
23	Xiamen	China	4,627,052
24	Tokyo	Japan	4,123,920
25	Jawaharlal Nehru (Nhava Sheva)	India	4,059,843
26	Dalian	China	3,813,300
27	Tanjung Priok	Indonesia	3,689,783
28	Gioia Tauro	Italy	3,445,337
29	Yokohama	Japan	3,428,112
30	Algeciras–La Linea	Spain	3,414,345
47[a]	Vancouver	Canada	2,307,289
57[a]	Seattle	USA	1,973,504
59[a]	Tacoma	USA	1,924,934
[b]	Prince Rupert	Canada	181,890

[a] Missing some rankings.
[b] These are 2008 figures because that was the first year of operation for the Port of Prince Rupert.
Source: AAPA 2009.

called the Aquatrain between Whittier, Alaska, and Prince Rupert, British Columbia. This has been in operation since 1962 and can be adapted to haul containers (Ladouceur 2009). These barges are operated by Foss Maritime for CN Railroad. There is an opportunity to establish an Aquatrain connection between southeast Alaska and Prince Rupert. In this case, freight from Ketchikan, Petersburg, Sitka, Wrangell, Craig, and other southeast locations would have to be consolidated in one location such as Ketchikan. The freight, once it enters Canada, is granted duty relief provided the container is exported within 30 days (Goodchild et al. 2008).

In 2008, forest products Asia-bound freight included containerized lumber, bulk logs, and wood pellets (table 9). However, there was very little forest products freight originating from Alaska owing to a lack of regularly scheduled barge service connecting southeast Alaska to the Port of Prince Rupert.

Table 9—Performance of Prince Rupert terminal, 2008

Terminal	Commodities	Quantity
		Metric tons
Fairview Terminal	Containers	1,800,000[a]
Prince Rupert Grain	Barley	443,482
	Canola	323,465
	Feed barley	0
	Grain screen	14,912
	Wheat	2,977,658
	Total	3,759,517
Ridley Terminal	Coal	4,109,428
	Coking coal	307,798
	Petroleum coke	358,404
	Wood pellets	71,401
	Total	4,847,031
Prince Rupert Harbor	Log	119,936

[a] Reported as 181,890 TEUs.
Source: Prince Rupert Port Authority 2009.

Conclusions

This paper summarized trends in the global shipping industry and their impact on Alaska. The Asian economy, led by China, is the engine pulling the world out of the global recession. Although U.S. forest markets remain sluggish, markets such as exports of western hemlock to South Korea are expanding. Many U.S. forest products companies have found themselves overly reliant on the U.S. market and their sales plunged along with U.S. credit and U.S. housing starts. One key lesson to be learned from this economic downturn is the importance of global markets. The U.S. forest products companies that export to Asia will be able to ride on the coattails of Asian economic growth. The following are the specific observations of this research:

- The value of the U.S. dollar has decreased against major Asian currencies. This makes Alaska forest products including Alaska yellow-cedar, western hemlock, and Sitka spruce more price competitive in Asia.

- Between 1997 and 2009, shipping rates for a 40-foot container of lumber fluctuated between about $680 and $1,325. As of November 2009, lumber shipping rates are about $800 per 40-foot container and, as the global economy improves, these rates could rise.

- The Ocean Shipping Reform Act of 1998 mandated that ocean carriers be allowed to set up private shipping contracts with customers. This allows exporters to negotiate lower ocean shipping rates if they can promise ocean carriers a larger volume of export shipments. Therefore, it would benefit Alaska exporters to develop a shipping cooperation that includes forest products and other exports. The goal would be to approach ocean carrier shipping companies such as COSCO with a high group export volume in order to negotiate favorable rates.

- There are limited intermodal connections from Alaska to Asia. Northland provides intermodal transport service through the Port of Seattle. They allow their containers to be loaded in Alaska and transferred directly onto ocean carriers bound for Asia, without unloading the containers. Some of the other barge lines do not allow their containers to go to Asia, so the cargo from these containers must be unloaded in Seattle (or another port) and reloaded into another container bound for Asia. This adds additional costs to shipping.

- One of the biggest developments in shipping that could affect Alaska forest products exporters was the opening of the Port of Prince Rupert in 2007. However, for Alaska's forest products industry to take advantage of Prince Rupert, scheduled barge service between southeast Alaska and the Port of Prince Rupert needs to be implemented. As of this writing, there is no barge service between southeast Alaska and Prince Rupert, so most of the containerized freight bound for Asia is barged farther south to either the Port of Seattle or the Port of Tacoma.

- The best potential barge service connecting southeast Alaska to Prince Rupert appears to be the Aquatrain barge, which is managed by the CN. The Aquatrain carries rail cars between Whittier, Alaska, and the Port of Prince Rupert, and can be retrofitted to carry shipping containers. However, there needs to be a coordinated effort among southeast Alaska exporters in all industries to demonstrate to CN that there is enough Asia-bound container volume to warrant a scheduled service.

Metric Equivalents

When you know:	Multiply by:	To find:
Inches (in)	2.5400	Centimeters (cm)
Feet (ft)	0.3048	Meters (m)
Miles (mi)	1.6090	Kilometers (km)
Acres (ac)	0.4050	Hectares (ha)
Log scale (mbf)	4.5000	Cubic meters, logs (m³)
Cubic meters, logs (m³)	0.222	Log scale (mbf)
Lumber (full sawn) (mbf)*	2.3600	Cubic meters, lumber (m³)
Cubic meters of lumber (m³)	0.4240	Lumber (full sawn) (mbf)*
Cubic meters of ALSC lumber (m³)	0.6200	ALSC dimension (mbf)**
ALSC dimension (mbf)	1.6140	Cubic meters of ALSC lumber (m³)
Pounds (lb)	0.4540	Kilograms (Kg)

---

* The normal basis for lumber volume in countries on the metric system is the cubic meter. This is based on nominal dimensions and shipping dry (12 to 20 percent) moisture content. This calculation applies only where the differences between nominal and manufactured sizes are negligible. It would not be appropriate in a case where American Softwood Lumber Standards were converted directly to metric equivalents, retaining the differences between nominal and manufactured sizes (Briggs 1994). Other sources: (Fonseca 2005, FAO 2010).

** Based on the assumption that the material is rough green and not in accordance with American Lumber Standard Committee (ALSC) regulations, a factor of 0.424 per mbf per m³ is used in this report. Given the statement by Briggs (1994) a factor of 0.620 per mbf per m³ is more appropriate for ALSC dimension lumber.

Literature Cited

Airline Deregulation Act of 1978; 49 U.S.C. Sect. 41713.

American Association of Port Authorities [AAPA]. 2009. World port rankings —2007. http://www.aapa-ports.org/Industry/content.cfm?ItemNumber= 900#Statistics. (November 23, 2009).

Bloomberg. 2010. Baltic Dry Index statistics. http://www.bloomberg.com/apps/ cbuilder?ticker1=BDIY%3AIND. (March 16, 2010).

Brackley, A.M.; Crone, L.K. 2009. Estimating sawmill processing capacity for Tongass timber: 2005 and 2006 update. Res. Note PNW-RN-561. Portland, OR: U.S. Department of Agriculture, Forest Service, Pacific Northwest Research Station. 15 p.

Brackley, A.M.; Nicholls, D.L.; Hannan, M. 2009. An evaluation of the grades and value of red alder lumber from southeast Alaska. Gen. Tech. Rep. PNW-GTR-774. Portland, OR: U.S. Department of Agriculture, Forest Service, Pacific Northwest Research Station. 27 p.

Brackley, A.M.; Haynes, R.W. 2008. Timber products output and timber harvests in Alaska: an addendum. Res. Note PNW-RN-559. Portland, OR: U.S. Department of Agriculture, Forest Service, Pacific Northwest Research Station. 41 p.

Briggs, D. 1994. Forest products measurements and conversion factors: with special emphasis on the U.S. Pacific Northwest. Institute of Forest Resources Contribution No. 75. Seattle, WA: University of Washington, College of Forest Resources. 161 p.

Brown, M.; Lui, P. 2009. Won crushes yen as dollar substitute in Asian rally. Bloomberg News Online. October 19. http://www.bloomberg.com/apps/news?pid=newsarchive&sid=ah6NVgkesLv4. (December 10, 2009).

Carson, J. 1989. Weights of building materials, agricultural commodities, and floor loads for buildings. Fact Sheet H-20. University Park, PA: Pennsylvania State University, Department of Agriculture. 4 p. http://www.age.psu.edu/extension/factsheets/h/H20.pdf. (December 22, 2009).

Creel, H.J. 2000. Remarks regarding the Posidonia Congress meeting in Athens, Greece. Press Release. Federal Maritime Commission. June 2. http://www.fmc.gov/speeches/newsrelease.asp?SPEECH_ID=50. (March 1, 2010).

Cunningham, K.H.; Eastin, I.L. 2002. Factors that influenced the export success of forest products companies in the Pacific Northwest during the 1997–1998 Japanese economic downturn. Working Paper 89. Seattle, WA: University of Washington, Center for International Trade in Forest Products. 57 p.

Donovan, A.; Bonney, J. 2006. The box that changed the world: fifty years of container shipping—an illustrated history. East Windsor, NJ: Commonwealth Business Media. 262 p.

Federal Maritime Commission. 2009. Shipping Act of 1984. http://www.fmc.gov/about/ShippingAct.asp. (October 9, 2009).

Federal Reserve Bank. 2010. Foreign exchange rates (monthly). http://www.federalreserve.gov/releases/g5/current/. (November 2010).

Fonseca, M.A. 2005. The measurement of roundwood-methodologies and conversion ratios. Wallingford, Oxfordshire, United Kingdom; Cambridge, MA. CABI Publishing. 269 p.

Food and Agriculture Organization [FAO] 2010. Forest products conversion factors for the UNECE Region. Geneva Timber and Forest Discussion Paper 49. UNECE/FAO Timber Section, Geneva, Switzerland. 38 p. http://timber.unece.org/fileadmin/DAM/publications/DP-49.pdf. (January 5, 2011).

Forsyth, R.W. 2009. Idle ships show global economy's dead in the water. Wall Street Journal Digital Network, Barron's. September 16. http://online.barrons.com/article/SB125305245885513721.html. (September 17, 2009).

Global Trade Information Services, Inc. [GTI]. 2009. Global trade atlas. http://www.gtis.com. (January 2010). On file with: Joseph A. Roos, University of Washington, Seattle, WA 98105.

Goodchild, A.; Albrecht, S.; Lam, T.; Faust, K. 2008. A container terminal at the Port of Prince Rupert: considerations from a transportation perspective. Canadian Political Science Review. 2(4): 60–75.

Halbrook, J.M.; Morgan, T.A.; Brandt, J.P.; Keegan, C.E., III; Dillon, T.; Barrett, T.M. 2009. Alaska's timber harvest and forest products industry. Gen. Tech. Rep. PNW-GTR-787. Portland, OR: U.S. Department of Agriculture, Forest Service, Pacific Northwest Research Station. 30 p.

Harlow, W.M.; Harrar, E.S. 1958. Textbook of dendrology. 4th ed. New York, NY: McGraw-Hill Book Company, Inc. 561 p.

Japan Customs Bureau. 2009. Export and import data. [Japanese]. http://www.customs.go.jp/toukei/srch/index.htm?M=01&P=0. (January 10, 2009).

Japan Wood-Products Information and Research Center [JAWIC]. 2009. Japan Wood Market Statistics. Tokyo: October. 26 p.

Kendall, L.C.; Buckley, J.B. 2001. The business of shipping. 7th ed. Centreville, MD: Cornell Maritime Press. 453 p.

Ladouceur, P. 2009. CN and the Port of Prince Rupert. [Presentation]. In: Southeast conference annual meeting. Haines, AK. September 15. http://www.seconference.org/pdf/Ladouceur%20-%20Haines_CN_Sept_15_2009.pdf. (March 1, 2010).

Nicholls, D.L.; Brackley, A.; Rojas, T. 2006. Alaska's lumber-drying industry—impacts from a federal grant program. Gen. Tech. Rep. PNW-GTR-683. Portland, OR: U.S. Department of Agriculture, Forest Service, Pacific Northwest Research Station. 23 p.

Nozawa, S. 2009. Dollar to hit 50 yen, cease as reserve, Sumitomo says. Bloomberg News Online. October 15. http://www.bloomberg.com/apps/news?pid=20601109&sid=a_A5nqmw9Dq8. (October 21, 2009).

Ocean Shipping Reform Act of 1998 [OSRA]; 46 App. U.S.C. 1701–1719.

Pacific Northwest Asia Shippers Association [PNASA]. 2009. Lumber shipping contract data. On file with: Joseph A. Roos, University of Washington, Seattle, WA 98105.

Port of Seattle. 2009. Seaport sailing schedule. http://www.portseattle.org/downloads/seaport/Seaport%20Sailing%20Sched.pdf. (December 28, 2010).

Port of Tacoma. 2009. Vessel schedule and rotation schedule. http://www.portoftacoma.com/Page.aspx?cid=2370. (December 28, 2010).

Prince Rupert Port Authority. 2009. Daily vessel report. http://www.rupertport.com/pdf/vesselschedule.pdf. (December 28, 2010).

Reuters. 2009. Seoul shares turn higher after GDP; drug firms rise. http://www.reuters.com/article/rbssFinancialServicesAndRealEstateNews/idUSSEO29491920091026. (October 29, 2009).

Roos, J.A.; Barber, V.; Sasatani, D.; Eastin, I. 2008a. The Japanese market for laminated lumber and glulam beams: implications for Alaskan forest products. Working Paper 113. Seattle, WA: University of Washington, Center for International Trade in Forest Products. 23 p.

Roos, J.A.; Sasatani, D.; Barber, V.; Eastin, I. 2008b. Trends in the Japanese forest products market and implications for Alaska forest products. Working Paper 114. Seattle, WA: University of Washington, Center for International Trade in Forest Products. 53 p.

Shipping Act of 1916; 46 App. U.S.C. 801 et seq.

Shipping Act of 1984; 46 App. U.S.C. 1702.

SR International Logistics. 2010. Standard containers. http://www.srinternational.com/standard_containers.htm. (March 1, 2010).

U.S. Department of Agriculture, Agricultural Marketing Service [USDA AMS]. 2009. Agricultural transportation—ocean rate bulletin [Database]. First quarter. http://www.ams.usda.gov/AMSv1.0/ams.fetchTemplateData.do?template =TemplateV&navID=AgriculturalTransportation&leftNav=Agricultural Transportation&page=ATORBArchive&description=Ocean%20Rate%20 Bulletin%20Database&acct=oceanfrtrtbltn. (March 1, 2010).

U.S. Department of Transportation, Federal Highway Administration [U.S. Department of Transportation FHA]. 2009. Bridge formula weights. http://ops.fhwa.dot.gov/freight/publications/brdg_frm_wghts. (October 15, 2009).

U.S. International Trade Commission [USITC]. 2009. Interactive tariff and trade dataweb. http://dataweb.usitc.gov/. (October 2, 2009).

Western Wood Products Association [WWPA]. 2005. Design values and spans for Alaska species lumber. Tech. Note TN05-01/Rev2-05. Portland, OR. 6 p.

Appendix—Sources for Global Shipping of Forest Products

American Forest & Paper Association
China Office
Director of Marketing: Xu Fang
Rm 4706, Tower 1 Grand Gateway
One Hangqiao Road
Tokyo 107-0052 JAPAN
200030 Shanghai, China
Tel: 86-21-6448-4401
Fax: 86-21-6448-4404
http://www.afandpa-china.org/

American Hardwood Export Council
U.S. Embassy 10F, 2-11-5
Nishi-Temma, Kita-ku, Osaka 530-0047
Tel: 81-6-6315-5101
Fax: 81-6-6315-5103
E-mail: info@ahec-japan.org
http://www.ahec.org/

Commercial Service of the U.S.
Japan
U.S. Embassy Tokyo
1-10-5 Akasaka,
Minato-ku, Tokyo 107-8420
Tel: 81-3-3224-5060
Fax: 81-3-3589-4235
E-mail:Tokyo.Office.Box@mail.doc.gov
http://www.buyusa.gov/japan/en/

Commercial Service of the U.S.
China
U.S. Embassy Beijing
No. 55 An Jia Lou Lu 100600
Tel: 86-10-8531-3000
E-mail:Tokyo.Office.Box@mail.doc.gov
http://www.buyusa.gov/china/en/

Export.gov
A list of export resources offered by the U.S. government.
http://www.export.gov/

JETRO
Japan External Trade Association
San Francisco Office
235 Pine Street, Suite 1700
San Francisco CA 94104
Phone: 415-392-1333
Fax: 415-788-6927

Japan Lumber Journal
25 Sankyo Bldg. No. 523
1-48-10, Higashi Ikebukuro,
Toshima-ku, Tokyo Japan 170-0013
Phone 81-3-5950-2251
Fax: 81-3-5950-2271
E-mail: njlj@scan-net-ne.jp
http://www.jlj.gr.jp/

The U.S./China Business Council
U.S. Office
1818 N Street, NW, Suite 200
Washington, DC 20036
Phone: 202-429-0340
Beijing Office
CITIC Building, Suite 10-01
19 Jianguomenwai Dajie
Beijing 100004, China
Tel: 86-10-6592-0727
http://www.uschina.org/

Softwood Export Council Japan Office
Edward Matsuyama
Tomoko Igarashi
AIOS Toranomon 9F
1-6-12 Nishi Shinbashi, Minato-ku,
Tokyo,105-0003, Japan
Tel: 03-3501-2131

The National Customer Brokers & Freight Forwarders Association of America
1200 18th Street NW No. 901
Tel: 202-466-0222
Fax: 202-466-0226
http://www.ncbfaa.org/

United States Department of Agriculture
Agricultural Marketing Service Ocean Rate Bulletin
Tel: 202-694-2505
http://www.ams.usda.gov/

www.ingramcontent.com/pod-product-compliance
Lightning Source LLC
Chambersburg PA
CBHW081137280526
45787CB00007B/3124